MY WALK WITH JESUS
Miracles in the Snow

HELEN R. BECHTEL

WINEPRESS  PUBLISHING

Printed in the United States of America

Packaged by WinePress Publishing, PO Box 1406, Mukilteo, WA 98275. The views expressed or implied in this work do not necessarily reflect those of WinePress Publishing. Ultimate design, content, and editorial accuracy of this work is the responsibility of the author(s).

ISBN 1-57921-151-8
Library of Congress Catalog Card Number: 98-61307

A Place Called Heaven

There is a place called heaven.
It's far beyond the blue.
With angels sweetly singing,
The old songs ever new.

The sun is always shining,
There's no night there, you see.
When the roll is called up yonder,
The Lord can count on me.

Heaven, oh, sweet heaven,
Blessed homeland of the soul.
We'll sing redemption's story,
While endless ages roll.

With John and Paul and Peter,
Our blessed Lord we'll see.
When the roll is called up yonder,
The Lord can count on me.

This glorious place called heaven,
It's a land of pure delight.
Where all the saints in glory,
Are dressed in garments white.

Up there, we'll meet our loved ones,
Around the glassy sea.
When the roll is called up yonder,
The Lord can count on me.

Oh, sinners, come to Jesus,
Come with your load of sin.
Christ died on Calvary's mountain;
He died your soul to win.

The Lord will surely pardon;
Your soul He will set free.
When the roll is called up yonder,
The Lord will call for thee.

To

Our Beloved Lord Jesus Christ

For walking with me throughout my life,
For giving me my miraculous experiences,
For giving me the precious gifts of
the miracle of His footprints,
and
For the blooming of my pussy willows and lilacs each
Christmas Day.
The Lord is my constant companion.
I love the Lord with all my heart.

Contents

The Lord Will Show You the Way

I have a true life journey and a miraculous experience to share with you, about how the Lord saved me from committing suicide and the wondrous gift He gave me.

In 1983 I went through a very traumatic divorce after twenty-eight years of marriage. My husband left me for a woman he worked with, which left me totally devastated. I just didn't want to live anymore. I felt betrayed by my mother, my father, and now my husband. All the people in my life I thought I could trust—they all betrayed me and left me alone. I felt as though someone had torn my heart out of my body and stomped on it. After a lifetime of hurt, I just didn't want to hurt anymore. During the first Christmas Eve alone, I considered suicide. I had the gun in my hand when the Lord spoke to me. He virtually took the gun away from me and told me He had something He wanted me to do for Him.

How does a person's life become so desolate and void of any reason for life to continue? A feeling so overwhelming, it feels like you're being suffocated. An emptiness and withering of spirit until you feel you are worth less than a grain of sand. An empty shell of a person devoid of all the reason, emotion, and sense of existing. The essence of life itself no longer a part of your existence.

Some people, hearing of a person's suicide, say, "How could they do it? End their own life? What about the people who love them so much? How could someone hurt their family and friends like that?" All really good questions! What people don't realize and can't comprehend is that the suicidal person already feels dead, simply existing in some kind of time warp. Sitting on the edge of the abyss, ready to plunge into the dark pit of no return. Not eating, not wanting to see anyone, just closing the windows and doors and wanting to be left alone. Isolating yourself from the world and from life itself. Sleeping—yes, sleeping is good. Sleeping allows your mind to completely shut down. You begin to think, *This must be what death is like, just endless sleep.* This thought becomes very real. Just going to sleep and not waking up!

That was my world.

What really happens with severe depression is that the brain chemistry actually changes. You become trapped in an undercurrent, pulling you down further and further until you are actually unable to help yourself. Only some kind of intervention will save you. This is exactly where I was—unable to help myself.

2

Snapshots of
My Childhood

I was never a very religious person. I grew up in a large
Catholic family. We all went to mass, but not every Sunday. I do know now that I have been walking with Jesus all
my life and have not realized it, because He is the only one
who could have protected me throughout the years.

When I was five years old, I lived in a housing project
called Miami Village Apartments, Fort Wayne Housing
Project. I lived with my mother, father, brothers, and sisters. We had a big family. Mom always seemed to be ex-
pecting another baby. My father was not very supportive of
the mother of his children. He was constantly seeing other
women, and my mother knew it. We were very poor—dirt
poor, as they say—because we could hardly afford soap.

I experienced my first real miracle when I was just five
years old. I was riding with my mother in a taxicab, and the

door flew open. I fell out of the cab and landed in front of the wheels. The cab stopped just in time, and I was saved. I had only some scrapes and bruises.

A family lived down the street from us. They had four children, and we played together. My mother became a good friend of this family. One day we saw an ambulance at their house. This was a rare and unusual occurrence in our neighborhood because everyone was too poor to go to the hospital for any reason. We all ran down to see what was happening. We stood in awe, staring, as they took the mother away. I felt very bad for my friends; they were very scared. We later heard she had a nervous breakdown and was sent to Richmond State Hospital. I never saw her again.

Then it seemed like all of a sudden, everything changed. One day my mother left and didn't come back. She moved in with this man, Harold, and his four children. I was so confused and scared. Their were seven of us children left without a mother. My oldest sister, Mary, was only thirteen years old. Ray was eleven, Jimmy was ten, I was seven, Johnny was four, Pam was two, and Judy was only a year old.

My father still lived with us, even though Mom was living with that other family. I don't think Daddy stayed to take care of us kids, as much as the fact that he had nowhere else to go. At one point, Mom told Daddy he had to leave the house, and he begged me to ask her to let him stay. I did talk to Mom, and she let him stay. I did feel my dad loved me. My mother never hugged or kissed me, but my dad gave me big hugs and kisses, and this meant so much to me. At night when I would be very scared and lonely, I would slip into bed with Daddy and curl up against him, and I would feel safe and secure. I can't tell you how much this supported and nurtured me. I was so starved for love and attention. I was Daddy's little girl. Dad was always good to me all my life.

We each had the clothes on our backs and one other change of clothes. So each night we had to handwash our clothes if we wanted something clean to wear to school the next day. All the other kids at school made fun of us constantly. The parish school we attended had wealthy families who would contribute clothes, coats, boots, shoes, etc. to us. Without this help, we all would have frozen to death walking to school in the winter. Of course, my oldest sister had to quit school to take care of the little ones and was put to work at an early age to bring home money for the family.

We lived in deplorable conditions, so it was really no wonder when we became infested with head lice. Mom found out, and she let Harold cut off all my hair. I was nearly bald. I was only eight years old and in the first grade at Saint Joseph's Catholic School. The first day I had to go back to school with my hair cut off, I wore a scarf. I didn't want the other kids to see my hair. I entered the classroom and took my seat, hoping no one would notice me. I wanted to just roll up in a little ball and close my eyes and pretend I was invisible. I couldn't believe it when the nuns immediately said I couldn't wear the scarf and made me take it off in the classroom in front of all the kids. This was one of the most humiliating things that ever happened to me. The other kids made fun of me constantly, and the nuns all acted like I was going to contaminate them.

It took forever for my hair to grow back. My heart still feels such sorrow and agony for the lost innocence of this little girl who was me. I don't think I will ever get over this episode in my life. I don't know why Mom did that to me. I was going through so much already, as an eight-year-old without my mother. I don't understand how a mother could allow her own child to be hurt. This was just one of many things Mom allowed Harold to do to me, and she said and did nothing to protect me.

The Blessed Mother of Jesus has always held a special place in my heart. When I was seven or eight years old, as I walked to school, I would stop and ask people for flowers for the Blessed Mother. I really believe the Blessed Mother was watching over us and gave us special graces to survive our childhood traumas.

I would sneak down to the garden Harold grew and steal tomatoes, potatoes, carrots, corn, turnips—anything I could find, because it seemed we were always hungry. Sometimes he would catch me in his garden and scare me away. He always called me bad names. But I didn't care; whenever I could, I would steal from his garden! It wasn't that I wasn't mortally afraid of him, because I was. It was really the fact that we needed the food, and I felt it was really a survival instinct that made me do it.

My mother would send food down for us to eat at suppertime each night, but it was never enough to feed all of us. We all really took care of ourselves. The older kids took care of the younger ones. Mom didn't even take the babies with her. She just left us to fend for ourselves.

When I would go down to their house to see my mother, Harold would get very mad and yell at me to go home, and he would always call me bad names. Mom did nothing to stop this. She just acted like it was normal for her to just leave us and move in with them. She didn't want the welfare people to know what was going on. She told us that if they found out, they would take us all away and we would not ever see each other again. We were so afraid they would take us away and put us in an orphanage, and we would never see our brothers and sisters again. Mom would tell us to say she was at the grocery store if anyone asked.

So no one ever knew we were alone and in desperate need of adult supervision and care. My father was not much of a father to any of us kids, but he seemed to show me the most attention and love. He would sometimes give me money when the ice cream truck came around. You can't imagine what a treat a simple popsicle is to a really poor child; it's like getting a precious gift.

My father loved his ham radios and would talk for hours to people on the radio. Daddy would let me talk to people also, and this made me feel special. His call letters were W9CXJ. He would spend all his money on his radio equipment and on himself, and never think twice about how his children were surviving. I wondered what was wrong with both my mother and my father. They both seemed to be in their own little worlds, and their worlds definitely did not include us.

One day a friend of his came to the house and Daddy told me to make them something to eat, but there was no food in the house. I told Daddy this, and he said, "That's OK, princess, we'll just go out and get something to eat." I couldn't believe he would go out to eat when his children had nothing to eat in the house.

The house was dirty, with cockroaches and mice everywhere. The summers were so miserably hot, and the winters were so incredibly cold. We had no fans to cool us in the summer. It was a magnificent treat, sent straight from heaven, when it rained. We loved playing out in the rain. It was truly a delight, and the child who got to the downspout first was the lucky one, because it was a torrent of blessed cool water. The winters, of course, were indescribable. We were all so cold all the time. None of the bedrooms had any heat; we would warm our blankets at the coal stove and run to bed. Getting up in the morning and getting dressed was terrible, but nothing like the torture of walking to school every day without proper winter clothes.

All of us kids just ran around all hours of the day and night. We had no supervision. No one really cared! We were all on our own, left to do whatever we wanted to do. It's truly a miracle that none of us were injured or killed. We played in the river under the bridge and walked the rapids. God must have held our hands. I didn't know how to swim and neither did any of my brothers or sisters. The Lord surely sent down a legion of guardian angels to protect all of us.

My father was looking for work out of town and was not home much. Our family just seemed to evaporate. It wasn't long before my parents were divorced. Then I had no mother and no father. My father didn't seem to care much what happened to us either. Like Mom, he just moved out, leaving us with no money, love, or attention from anyone except each other. He soon moved out of the state and was afraid to even come and see us at all, because my mother said she would have him arrested for not paying any child support.

I took care of myself and tried to take care of my younger brothers and sisters the best I could. Soon the rent was not being paid at our house or at the house Mom was at. So the landlord evicted us. Now we were without a mother, a father, or a home. We had to go to a halfway house called the Wayne Township Transient Annex, and plans were being made to send us to the orphanage at Saint Vincent's Villa. Since Mom could not send us alone, Harold and his kids went with us. Just one big unhappy family.

My oldest sister, Mary, my brother Jimmy, my sisters Pam and Judy, and baby Joe all went to live with a friend of my mother's. We called her Aunt Midge. The lady who ran the shelter, Mrs. Hogan, was incredibly wonderful to us. She would cook us big delicious meals and keep us clean, warm, and dry. She was the one bright star in my life, and the Lord surely sent her down from heaven to care for us, because even at the shelter, Mom was never there.

We lived at the Transient Annex for a year before we finally had a home again. By now we were one big integrated family, but we always felt like outsiders. You would think this would have been a better life, but that was not in the cards for us.

We moved to a house on Webster Street. It was only four rooms downstairs and one large room upstairs, but you had to go to an outside stairway to get upstairs. Of course, the upstairs room became the room for about eight girls. It was very frightening to go outside at night to go to bed. One day my little sister fell down those steps and broke her collarbone. There was no heat in this room, and we all huddled together in bed to keep from freezing to death.

My stepfather was a drunk and mean to all of us. My mother worked at the Saint Vincent DePaul Society's secondhand store, mostly to be able to get us clothes and other necessities. It seemed like my mother was never home, so again we raised ourselves. We now lived in a house with thirteen kids: four of his, seven of hers, and by now they had two more together. Including my mother and stepfather, we had fifteen people living in a five-room house.

My mother had some strict rules, and one of these rules was that none of the girls could share clothes, jewelry, etc. She did not want to have anyone fighting over possessions. As a matter of fact, all of us kids were to be seen and not heard. Mom was particularly proud when someone came to visit and there were sixteen kids in the house but the visitors could never tell it, because we were so quiet.

In truth, we were all scared to death to make a noise. Mom did not allow any fighting or bickering among us kids. If the very rare occasion of a fight or disagreement would happen, Mom was always the one who settled it, usually with a belt or a switch from a tree. Mom would say to the offender, "Come here!" If you ran away from her, you would get whipped twice as hard, so we all learned to come when called.

Also, with so many mouths to feed, we ate lots of potatoes, spaghetti, and bread—anything that would stretch a long way. We ate a lot of government surplus food, like powdered eggs, cheese, powdered milk, and butter. I still remember the taste of French toast made from powdered milk, powdered eggs, and day-old bread. Mom would also do a lot of home canning of vegetables from the garden.

In my mother's defense, I know she did love us all very much, and she had a terrible life herself. I'm sure she was just trying to get us all to survive. Sometimes Mom would try to do special things for us kids. She had very little money, but she would try and bring us home little treats. We always looked forward to the times Mom went to the grocery store, which weren't very often. She would bring us each a little, individual half pint of ice cream. It looked just like a big carton of ice cream, but it was tiny, and she always brought us cherry vanilla flavor, with real chunks of cherries in it. After I got married, I would almost make myself sick eating so much cherry vanilla ice cream. This doesn't sound like much, I know, but to us it meant so much.

When I was growing up, it was a strange thing, but I always knew things before they happened. When I was twelve, my mother was pregnant, and I knew the baby was a boy, and I knew he was dead before he was born. When he was born dead, I had to give him a bath and dress him and get him ready for the undertaker. This was very hard for me to do. I cried and cried. I had never seen a dead person before, much less my own baby brother.

Mom named him Junior. He weighed seventeen pounds at birth. Other than being very large for a newborn, he was a remarkably beautiful baby. He had jet black hair, and it was very long and thick. He was truly an angel. After I dressed him, Mom wanted to hold him. She held him, and big tears rolled down her face as she kissed him and said goodbye. We shared the grief of losing him together, and I felt very close to my mother for the first time in my life. I wanted so much to tell him how much we loved him; I just kissed his little head and gave him to the undertaker. The doctor said he died because he had an enlarged heart.

After the undertaker came and got the baby, I stayed up all night taking care of my mom. She was hemorrhaging, and I was afraid we would lose her also. I prayed to the Lord Jesus to help Mom, and she got better.

We had no heat, no running water, and only a outhouse to go to the toilet. Mom would heat water on the potbellied stove in the living room and fill a small tub of water to bathe all the kids. She would start with the youngest and end with the oldest child, then wash herself, all with the same water.

I always got straight Fs in school, because I couldn't see and we never had any money for glasses. I would do babysitting, but Mom always took all the money I made. Most of the dirty work always fell on the oldest female in the house. My mother took me out of school when I was fourteen to take care of my brothers and sisters. I was only in the seventh grade. I never did get to go back to school.

Mom lied to the school and told them I went to live with my aunt in Kentucky. After this I could not be seen, so I could not ever go outside. The neighbors might see me and report Mom. I knew if I was seen by anyone, Mom would be in a lot of trouble for taking me out of school. I had to hide when anyone came to the door.

I felt like I was in prison. It was terrible because it was like I didn't exist anymore. I had no friends and couldn't see anyone except family. It was no wonder that at the age of fifteen I had had enough and just wanted out of this situation. I was not getting along well with my stepfather, and since I didn't go to school with the other kids, I couldn't go anywhere. I felt miserable all the time.

3

Moments Frozen in Time

I dated a boy by the name of Dale for a year. He was a wonderful person, and I should have married him. I loved Dale, but he didn't want to get married, because I was so young.

So I started dating other people, and I met John. I thought I loved him. I guess I really married him to get out of the bad life I had at home. I thought I would finally have a home of my own, a man who loved me, and children to love. I didn't know I was jumping straight into the fire. I thought it was bad at home with my stepfather and mother—well, it was just the beginning of my hell.

When I met John, I should have known something was wrong. He did not like to show affection. We never kissed or held hands like other couples. But I was just a child myself; I really didn't know much about anything. All I knew for sure was that I wanted out of the house. After we were married, John said he married me because his dad told him he would never find a "good girl" to marry. So he showed his dad he had a good girl. I know now we both got married for the wrong reasons.

John and I were married on August 6, 1955, and immediately I knew I was in trouble. I was so very young, only sixteen, and I had never lived or experienced anything. I hadn't ever been in a grocery store or restaurant before I married John. I felt very out of place and lost. John was never home. I found out later he had other women and was into doing drugs and getting in with the wrong kinds of people. I didn't know what to do, except to stay and hope that John would change, but he never did!

John and I had two beautiful daughters, but this did not change anything. When I was in the hospital having Joann and Cathy, he didn't stay with me. He had to be with his buddies, doing his own thing. He was never home, and just like when I was growing up, I was alone and abandoned. It was just me and my girls.

John would leave the house every weekday morning at 6:00 A.M. for work and would return home promptly every night at 6:00 P.M., even though his workday ended at 3:00 P.M. On weekends he would say he was going to get the car washed or going to the gas station or to get a haircut—all kinds of excuses. He would leave the house by 8:00 A.M., and he wouldn't return home until around 6:00 P.M. It became somewhat of a joke between my daughters and myself that he would be at the all-day car wash or be getting an all-day haircut. It would be years before I found out that he was into drugs and seeing other women.

I always longed for a real home, with a mother and a father living together and being a real family. I think this is why I stayed with John for so many years: I wanted my daughters to have a mother and a father and a family life. So I put up with John never being home, the other women, and the drugs. He made my life hell on earth.

When he was put into jail, the hurt and humiliation I felt were unbearable. One time he was put in jail and I had to take my oldest daughter, Cathy, to the jail with me to get him out. This was an awful thing for a little girl to see. But John didn't care about his wife or kids; he thought only of himself and did exactly what he wanted to do. He always put himself first.

One good thing during those years was that I became closer to my mother. We were both having babies at the same time. My youngest sister was born about the same time as my own daughter Cathy. So they played a lot with each other. I guess I now had more in common with my mother. As time passed, Mom became fiercely protective of her children, like a grizzly bear protecting her cubs. She was also an extremely possessive and controlling mother. She wanted things her way and would do anything to get what she wanted.

As the years passed, my oldest sister and two oldest brothers were married also. We did become very close to Mom and Harold. Every Sunday, Mom would make big dinners for all of us. Mom loved cooking and preparing large meals. She would have two or three kinds of meat, mashed potatoes, her world-famous chicken and noodles, etc. I think she tried to overcompensate for all the poor, lean years by making such big meals when things were good. We would bring pies, cakes, etc., but she would make most of the food. We would all spend the whole day at home.

We would also take vacations together. One vacation was to the Smoky Mountains. We all had a wonderful time. Most of the kids were young and had never experienced anything so wonderful as staying at a motel and swimming in a pool.

We stopped at all the sightseeing places. One of those places was Rock City. It had a trail to walk through the rock formations. My mother was a large woman, and one of the rock formations was called "Fat Man's Squeeze." Well, my mother thought she could make it through this, so she tried and got stuck. She was laughing so hard that it only made things worse. We were all trying to get her out. I was worried, but Mom was just laughing hysterically, so she got us all laughing. The guys were teasing Mom, saying that they were going to have to grease her up to get her out. Of course, she got out all by herself.

Then we got to a swinging bridge. Mom started over the bridge, and my brothers started swinging it. Mom was laughing and trying to hold on. Mom always carried a big black purse, and she almost dropped it over the side. She was a great one for carrying single, one-dollar bills; and she had about 300 dollars in her purse. We laughed to think of her purse coming open and all those ones floating to the ground. I really appreciate having some wonderfully good memories of Mom and my family.

Mom became a very giving person and considered no one a stranger. She would help anyone, and her family came first. When my daughter Joann was six months old, we lived out in the country, and we had only one car. One day Joann was extremely sick and John didn't come home to take her to the doctor. I prayed and prayed for the Lord to help my baby. I was so scared. She was having trouble breathing, and her color didn't look right. That night, my sister and mother came over to see her. My mother took one look at Joann and said she thought Joann had pneumonia. She called the doctor, and he said to bring her immediately to the hospital. She had double pneumonia. The doctor said she would have been dead by morning if we had not gotten her to the hospital that night.

If John had been home the way he should have been, I could have gotten the baby to the doctor before she got so bad. He really didn't even seem concerned. I believe the Lord heard my urgent plea for help through my prayers and sent my mother and sister that night, or my baby would have died. Joann lives today because the Lord was there to save her. Both my daughters, Joann and Cathy, love the Lord very much.

Another episode happened when Joann was four years old. She was barefoot outside and stepped on glass and actually cut her toe off. There was blood all over the kitchen, and I could not clean it up before rushing her to the hospital. I took her to the hospital, and the doctor saved her toe by suturing it back on. John came home and saw all the blood in the kitchen but was not even curious about what happened. He left and went out to eat. He didn't even call anyone to see what happened. He didn't care! This is what I put up with just so my daughters had a part-time father. Any man can be a sperm donor; it takes a real man to be a good father.

By the time my daughters were both married and had families of their own, I thought finally John and I would grow closer. I would make him special meals and keep the house neat and clean. I would not nag at him about where he was going or when he would be back. I just sat and waited for him to change and everything to be good.

But he only got worse. Now he was staying out all night, not calling or even telling me where he was. I would sit by the window all night and cry, waiting to see his car head-lights pull into the drive. He would never take me any-where or show me any affection. I was so alone. I found out later that John would take women up to our lake cottage, and he would introduce them to our neighbors as his sis-ters. John had no sisters. Again, I couldn't believe the things he did to me.

One day he came home, ate supper, then told me he wanted a divorce. He moved out into his own apartment. He was seeing another woman; her name was Irene, and she was married. I found out later from my daughter Joann that John and Irene had been having an affair for twelve years. I can't imagine a father telling his daughter about his affairs. The strange thing was that after John got his divorce, Irene dumped him and started seeing someone else. I thought that was at least some kind of justice.

I really could not believe my life; it was like some kind of nightmare. I didn't think John really meant it when he asked me for a divorce, but he did. We were divorced in 1983, after being married for twenty-eight years. I didn't think John would really get a divorce, because he had everything a man could ever want: a good wife; two wonderful, beautiful daughters; and terrific grandchildren—a real family who loved him. He also had a home, a place at the lake, and two new cars; and we both had good jobs, which meant financial security. Just when life was supposed to be happy and stable, he took away my life and everything I loved—a real family life.

It was so strange and frightening to be alone. Even though John was never supportive of me or our two girls, I felt like I could not live without him. He was so cold toward me and the kids all the time, never showing us any love and always going away from us, leaving us alone. At least, back then, I had the girls with me—but now I was truly alone, and it was devastating. It's hard to think about all the bad things that happened to me and my daughters.

John could have made it so much better. It sounds crazy, but even though he was unfaithful to me, I did not want a divorce. I didn't want him to leave me all alone. I felt so betrayed and heartbroken by this man, who was my whole life for so many years. Two daughters: Cathy and Joann; five grandchildren: Destiny, Brandy, Cristin, Cheryl, and

Trevor; and one great-grandson, Braton, are the only good things that came out of that marriage.

In 1983 the divorce was final, but I still could not accept it. I would bake John cookies, cakes, pies, or whole meals and leave them on his porch. I was hoping he would change his mind and come back home. I would buy him roses and leave them for him in his car at work or on his porch, but he always treated me so badly.

I loved John; he was my whole life. Even after the divorce, I tried to include him in our lives. He was invited for the kids' and grandkids' birthdays and for holidays like Thanksgiving and Christmas. We even took vacations together and had a good time. We loved each other, but he had to have his own life.

John moved to Arizona for two years. I went on a vacation to Arizona and stayed with him for a week. John took me to the Grand Canyon and showed me all around Arizona. It was hard to leave him there and come home. The morning John took me to the airport, he cried and I cried too. We talked on the phone all the time. He lost his job in Arizona and was living on the street in a box. He said he had to fight over the box to sleep in each night. Why did he give up everything he had with his family to live in a box? I still don't know why John would mess up his own life.

It got really bad for him, so he called his daughter Joann and asked to come back to Fort Wayne and live with her. She told him, "Dad, get back here where you belong, with us and the grandkids." Cathy also told him he could live with her family. The grandkids didn't even know him, but

Joann was so glad he was coming home. She thought he was finally going to straighten out his life and become responsible.

John did get to know his grandkids again. He lived with Joann for three months. He came back home on December 10 and was home for Christmas. I went to Joann's house for Christmas, and he was glad to see me. Cathy and her two children were there also. For one day, we were a real family again.

After three months with Joann, he came to live with me. If you can believe it, I thought he was home for good, but he wasn't. He was just using me to get back on his feet. He was the same as before, staying out all night, coming and going as he wished. He should have been different, but he wasn't. He didn't appreciate being home and being taken care of.

Soon I couldn't take it any longer, so I made him move out. Even when he was in his own apartment, I tried to take care of him, bringing him food and other things. But he told everyone I was harassing him and I wouldn't leave him alone. So I finally had to accept the fact that he was not a part of my life anymore. This threw me into a deep depression. I didn't want to live!

It was especially difficult as the first Christmas alone drew near. Christmas was really the only time we seemed to draw close as a family. It was always a very special time of the year for me and the girls. I always loved the holidays. I made big dinners every Thanksgiving and Christmas. I just loved family life, but he took it away from me when he left.

When John found out he had leukemia, I would take food over to his apartment for him. One day he told me he was hungry for my meat salad. I made him some and took it over to him. The day was very windy and he would not answer the door, so I left it inside his screen door. Later I was at my daughter Joann's house and the phone rang. She answered it, and it was John. He told her that I was there and trying to break into his apartment. Joann said, "I don't think so, Dad. Mom is talking to me here at my house right now." It was just the wind banging his door back and forth, and he thought it was me trying to break in. He just said, "Oh." Joann told him to go and get his meat salad, and he went to the door and found it. We just laughed and said, "What's wrong with him?"

I tried to forgive John before he died. I brought him roses, fruit, and his favorite McDonald's milkshakes at the hospital. John lived for two years after being diagnosed with cancer. I was hoping he would get on the right side with the Lord before he died, but I don't think he did, because he never made any attempt to make amends with his family. When he was dying he did not ask for me or Joann or Cathy. He died a lonely old man by himself. The day of his funeral, my daughters, grandchildren, and I were not there. That is the way he wanted it.

My life has always been hard but so have my daughters' lives. I have had to help Cathy and Joann with things that happened to them in their lives. They are still paying the price of not having a father around for support and affection. The girls needed their father very much. Joann asked Cathy, "Did you ever cry when Dad died?"

Cathy said, "No, did you?"

Joann said, "No, I never cried either. I cried enough over Dad when I was growing up." I think this is so sad for John that his own daughters did not care when he died.

John missed out on so much—not only his daughters, but his grandchildren. Cathy, Joann, and my grandchildren and great-grandson keep me going every day. They need me, and I need them. I know my girls love me, and I love them. I know Joann and Cathy would cry and miss me if I died. I have always been there for them all their lives.

John's neighbor at the apartment told me that John had told him he knew I loved him. Why didn't John tell *me*? It would have meant so much to me. I'm glad his neighbor told me, because it really made me feel good. I always loved him, no matter what he did. I try to think about some of the good times John and I had. We took some wonderful trips together, especially one out west. That is really God's country, just so beautiful.

I think, in his own way, John did love me and his daughters but honestly did not know how to show it. John had a bad life too. His mother left him with his father when he was four weeks old. John asked me once, "Why didn't my mother want me, Helen?" I didn't have an answer for him. I couldn't understand why my mother had abandoned me, so how could I know why his mother left him?

I can understand why John was never affectionate. He never had anyone to love him as a child, so he was never exposed to love. He never learned what love was or how to show it. His father was mean to him. When John was only a year old, he touched a red-hot potbellied stove and his hand was severely burned. His father never even took him to the doctor or put a bandage on it. I can imagine how much that injury hurt, and he didn't have any pain medication or anything. He had a scar on his hand. His father never showed any love for John; he beat him all the time.

I did think that John would change because I was showing him love, but I guess it was too late for him to learn how to love and care for someone else. I think being abandoned by his mother scarred his heart forever, like the burn scarred his hand. If you lose your mother as a baby, it will have a severe effect on your life. It causes you to have problems with attachment disorder. You really never learn how to attach your feelings to someone. The bad things that happen to you leave lasting imprints on your mind, even though you may want to forget and forgive. It's like being haunted by your past.

John did have a stepmother, but she was very evil. She would beat him with her cane. When John was four years old, his dad was out of town and his stepmother, Vernal, was taking care of him. She beat John so much that he stayed in the barn for two days until his dad got back.

John never had birthday cake until he married me. Also, he had never had a Christmas. John said that when he was little, Christmas was just another day. How can people treat little kids like this? I do blame John's mother and father for the way he was with his own kids and me. I hope and pray the Lord forgave him and he is in heaven now. I also hope he has found peace and happiness.

As the days passed and Christmas drew closer and closer, I became totally despondent and was thinking of suicide almost continuously. My state of mind was deteriorating rapidly. The depression was like a black cloud totally encompassing my brain. Since 1983 when John left me, I feel like I have been to hell and back. When John left I truly didn't want to live.

When we were married we became one person. As Genesis says, "Therefore shall a man leave his father and his mother, and shall cleave unto his wife: and they shall be one flesh." (Gen. 2:24 KJV). I really felt that John had taken half of me away. No one can live as half a person. I felt like I was stripped of the life force or spirit and soul of a person.

4

My Miracle

During that first Christmas Eve alone, I was beyond reason, and suicide seemed like the only answer for me. I felt my life was over. I sat with the gun in my hand. I stared out the window and watched the twilight come. It seemed like I sat there for a lifetime, motionless, as the snapshots of my life passed before me—first my childhood, then my marriage, . . . my children. Joann's and Cathy's husbands had both left them too. All three of us were divorced in the same year. How could this happen to all of us? Really, my whole life passed before my eyes, like a parade of unbelievable passages from a novel. My mind saw pictures, and events of my whole life unfold before me until I could not bear to see or hear or feel any of the memories anymore.

I became very frightened and frantically tried to take the bullets out of the gun—trying to somehow come to grips with myself, to possibly become sane again. But the devil did not want me to change my mind. He would not let the bullets come out of the gun, and I kept hearing, *Do it! Do it! Just get it over with, and you won't feel all this pain anymore.* That was screaming in my head constantly.

I felt so alone and in pain, as if I was suffering so much, I couldn't stand to feel all the hurt I had experienced in my whole life. It felt like my heart had been taken out and stomped on. My heart hurt so bad. I thought my heart was going to explode from the sorrow I felt. I cried hysterically for a long time. Then it was like I went limp and nothing seemed to matter anymore. I was empty, void of all emotion. Then I knew I could really do it. I felt the gun in my hand. It felt reassuring, and I lifted the gun slightly to my head. I said, "Lord, forgive me. I just can't do it anymore. I want out of here!"

In the next instant, I heard a new voice in my head—a reply to my invitation for the Lord to intervene. I heard a kind, loving voice, and a presence came over me. Somehow I knew it was the Lord. The Lord Jesus virtually took the gun from my hand and said, *"I have a plan for your life. You will not do this. You will become one of My people and a voice for My plan."*

He did not tell me what His plan was. I got up and took a bath and went to bed. I talked to the Lord and told Him how miserable and alone I was. I told Him I would need help to want to live again. I lay in bed and felt alone, afraid, and in despair. I asked the Lord to give me a hug, and I could feel His arms around me, and then I felt better and not alone anymore. I fell into a deep sleep.

5

Footprints in the Snow

I n the night, I felt a great heat all over my body, then penetrating into my body. I tried to open my eyes, but I couldn't. I was being filled with the Holy Spirit, and felt a peace and serenity that I had never known before. I heard the wind getting stronger and stronger, like from a distance, then upon my house. The windows rattled, and the house shuddered as though it were engulfed in a tornado. I became frightened and thought the wrath of God must be upon me. The words of the poem "Footprints" came to me from somewhere in my mind. I concentrated on the Lord and kept thinking over and over, *In the worst times in my life He would be carrying me, thus only one set of footprints in the sand.* This comforted me very much, and I fell into an extremely peaceful sleep.

When I got up the next morning, it was Christmas Day, and I felt wonderfully at peace. I felt so much better. I knew the Lord was in control of my life. I went into the kitchen and started to run some water in the pot for coffee. I looked out the kitchen window and there, in the snow, I immediately saw the footprints. I had the poem "Footprints in the Sand" hanging on my kitchen wall. I stared at it and read the verse, and immediately knew that the Lord had carried me during the night. I couldn't believe it at first. It was truly a miracle to believe in. The Lord had left me a sign of His presence—something for me and the world to see—a visible sign of His visit to me.

I went outside, and I didn't feel cold at all. The footprints in the snow were so wonderful—a sign from our Heavenly Father that He is truly with us always and carrying us when we are lost and alone. The footprints were only around the tree in a circle. There were no footprints leading to the tree or away from it.

I looked around in amazement. Then I saw more miracles in my yard! My pussy willow bush and lilac bush were blooming. It was beautiful. Then I noticed that my Blessed Mother statue was gone. The Blessed Mother has always been a special part of my life, and I had this statue in my yard for many years. It really seemed like the heavy statue had just vanished, because there were no footprints in that area of the yard where the statue had been—only a pure white blanket of snow. I called my brother and my sister, and they came out to see my miracle of the footprints. My sister took pictures of the footprints, and I took some also.

Mom had a Christmas party that day, and I went and told everyone about the footprints and the flowers blooming. I had not spoken to my brother Ray for over twenty years, but at the Christmas party I spoke to him and told him that I forgave him for the things he had done to me in the past. I went up to him and hugged him, and he almost fainted. He asked everyone, "What happened to Helen?"

On December 26, 1986, my flowers were in full bloom and I knew the Lord wanted the world to see this miracle. I called the television station WPTA Channel 21, and they sent out a film crew and a reporter to document this strange phenomenon. My bushes were in full bloom—and there was snow on the ground and freezing temperatures. I told the photographer about the footprints. I was afraid he would step on them, so I told him not to walk in that part of the yard. He said it was a miracle, but they never took any pictures of the footprints.

The Channel 21 News authorities wanted to verify this mystery of the blooming plants, and they contacted the local Allen County Agricultural and Horticultural Cooperative Extension Service Office, which is located at Indiana Purdue University in Fort Wayne, Indiana. The specialists were not able to explain why this miracle was happening, and told the reporters that the plants were "out of their natural cycle." At this point, I knew the Lord had really worked a miracle, not only for me to see, but for all His people to see and witness. I was on Channel 21 News with my flowers on December 26, 1986.

In the months to come, the fog around me seemed to lift. I let the Lord lead my life. This doesn't mean I wasn't still lonely, but whenever I found myself really feeling sad and hopeless, I would ask the Lord to give me a hug and hold me. I could feel His arms around me, and I felt a lot better about myself and not so alone anymore. I had much better self-esteem. I prayed from the Bible each night and waited to see what the Lord wanted me to do.

One day, I was at the pet store and I saw a large white angelfish. It was the most beautiful fish I had ever seen. I knew I just had to take this fish home, but the man did not want to sell it, because it was so unusual. He said he had never seen such a pure white fan-tailed angelfish before. I begged him to sell me the fish, and he finally agreed. I don't know why, but I felt like I just had to have that fish.

I took him home and put him in my aquarium. I would turn off the lights, and just the aquarium light was on. It seemed like he would swim right up and look at me. There was just something strange and wonderful about his eyes. I know it sounds crazy, but he brought a special peace and tranquility to my home. I felt this fish was special and was a form of the Holy Spirit. My sisters would come to my house, and they both said how peaceful they felt when watching my special white fish. It was like he could bring you into a calming trance.

In February, my beautiful fish developed a red wound on his side. My sister said it reminded her of the piercing wound our Lord suffered at the crucifixion. On February 1, 1984, I started feeling sick. I thought I had a cold. I was feeling strange. I had a feeling something was going to happen, but I didn't know why I felt that way. Then, on February 6, my wonderful white fish died. I had had him for three months.

I feel this white fish somehow had something to do with everything that was happening. I felt very sad and thought I would have to bury him because I couldn't think of just flushing him down the toilet like I had with other fish that died. I was thinking about burying him when I heard the Lord tell me to put the fish on a paper and place it in the pussy willow bush. I did not question this. It was dark outside, and I usually did not go outside after dark, but I did as the Lord wanted. I took my fish out and put it in the pussy willow bush. I cried and cried because something I loved was taken from me again. I felt a real peace when I had the fish in my house.

6

Heaven
and Hell

The next day, I wanted to see my fish one last time. I
went out to the pussy willow bush and looked everywhere, but the fish and the paper I put him on were both
gone. For the next few days, I continued to feel sick and
left work even though I could not afford to lose the money.
On February 8, I left work early at 9:00 A.M., and the next
day I couldn't go to work at all. That night I felt strange. I
was very tired and did not feel well. I sat in the chair, and
my arm and chest were hurting. I got my furry blanket off
my bed and lay down on the floor in my living room for a
while. I got back up and sat in the chair again. The pain
grew more intense. I thought I should call someone, but
again a voice said, *"Everything will be all right."* The pain
came again, but by now it was a crushing pain in my chest.
I knew I was having a heart attack! I was panic-stricken

and could hardly breathe for a few seconds, but then the Lord told me not to be afraid, and the pain was relieved somewhat.

The Lord told me to read Isaiah 13:21–22. I opened my Bible, and it seemed to immediately open up to the right page. I read the passage: "But wild beasts of the desert shall lie there; and their houses shall be full of doleful creatures; and owls shall dwell there, and satyrs shall dance there. And the wild beasts of the islands shall cry in their desolate houses, and dragons in their pleasant palaces; and her time is near to come, and her days shall not be prolonged." When I finished reading this passage, I knew I was dying, and I was greatly afraid. The Lord said, *"Close your eyes, and do not fear; trust in Me and everything will be all right."* Then He took me with Him.

I had no pain now. I felt only warmth, peace, and love surround me. Then I was in heaven with the Lord. He told me things He wanted me to do for Him. My body was here on earth, but my heart, mind, soul, and spirit were in heaven with the Lord. He said, *"Tell the people, I am coming back soon for my people. This will happen by the year 2000."*

I was on the other side for three months, and the Lord was telling me what to do for Him. When I was with the Lord, He told me not to wear the color black, not to drink coffee, not to use any form of birth control, and not to smoke or drink alcohol. He made me get a trash bag and put all of those things in the trash. The Lord did not explain why; I just did it without questioning Him. I changed my ways for the one and only true God, whom I love. I feel He was purifying my body, mind, spirit, and soul. I would sit in the bathtub for long periods with the water running over me. The water was also purifying and very tranquil.

The Lord told me secrets about my family. The Lord made me love my husband and everyone else who had ever hurt me, even when I didn't want to love anyone at that time. During that time, my granddaughter Brandy had a kidney problem, and the doctors said she would need surgery. She had two tubes leading to her kidneys instead of one. I prayed for her, and she was healed by the power of the Holy Spirit and the Lord Jesus. Brandy went back to the doctor, and he took new X-rays. One of the tubes was pinched off. The doctors said it was a miracle and Brandy did not need the surgery. I now call Brandy "my miracle baby."

I told John about the Lord to get him to turn his life around before he died. I don't know if he ever did make peace with the Lord. I pray he did. I want all people to feel the presence of the Lord in their lives and accept God into their lives. Only in this way will they enter the peace of heaven. I was in heaven with the Lord, and everyone should want to go there and be in heaven with our Lord.

I can tell you where heaven is. It is the North Star. I was there for three months with the Lord. The Lord is pure love; I felt a peace and love I never felt before. When my spirit and soul were with the Lord, my physical body on earth glowed with health. My fingernails and hair did not grow. I did not eat much and lost a lot of weight. I was only a shell of a person, a spirit on this earth, while actually I was on the other side in heaven with the Lord.

The Lord looks just like the pictures you see of Him. He has long brown hair, wonderfully warm brown eyes, and a beard. When you look at His picture, know you are seeing the true Lord Jesus. I have seen the face of Jesus and He looks just like all of the pictures handed down throughout the ages.

Love, joy, and resounding happiness permeate your existence in heaven. The Lord radiates such warmth and love. It would be impossible to put it into words because no words can explain or describe it. It's like the most brilliant light you've ever seen. He draws you to Him, and you never want to leave.

The Lord also showed me hell. I heard people moaning and moaning, like they were in terrible, constant pain. He showed me every bad thing I ever did in my life. All of the sins in my life flashed before my eyes. I can tell you I am not that other Helen now. I'm glad I'm not, because I know I would go to hell when I die. The people in hell are tormented constantly and unbearably. It was horrible to hear the people moaning loudly and crying out for salvation. My heart and prayers went out to them.

If you are ever in doubt about whether there is a hell or not, believe me, there is a hell. It is very real. I saw hell, and I was terrified. The moaning and crying were actually so loud, I told them to be quiet. I couldn't stand to hear it. I do not want to ever see anyone go to hell. You cannot even imagine the suffering and grief the souls have to endure in hell, and it is forever!

My dad once told me that when he was very sick with kidney failure, he died and saw hell. He said it was all fire, and he could hear terrible moaning and screaming. When I said, "Really?" as though I didn't believe him, he became very mad at me and said it was true. He really did experience hell. I think the Lord was giving him a second chance to change his life. My father lived for two years after this experience and did change. He was more religious and carried a rosary of Our Blessed Mother on his belt constantly. When he was in the hospital and dying, he was at peace.

God gives people time to change their ways. He gave John a lot of time to change. I hope he did.

Heaven is the most beautiful place you could ever imagine. Heaven is very peaceful and has a strong feeling of unconditional love and acceptance. Our loving, merciful Lord wants all His people to know there is a life after death. The Lord Jesus is all love, all caring, and all knowing. The Lord loves all His people.

My Mission for the Lord

W hen the time did come for me to come back here, I was sitting in the chair and the Lord said He had to leave me now. He said, *"I will always be here for you. Never forget I am here whenever you need me."*

I said, "No, please, Lord, do not leave me here. I want to stay with you!" I cried and sobbed. I begged Him, and I didn't want the Lord to leave me here. I wanted to go back with Him and stay with Him forever. But He told me again that there were things He wanted me to do for Him. I couldn't bear for Him to leave me, and I begged Him to stay. He blessed me and said, *"Remember My words."*

I can still see Him, for He walks with me; I can still feel Him, for He stirs within my heart; I can still hear His words ringing strong and true. I will never be the same since that moment in time, when He became a part of my heart. For the first time in my life, I looked into His eyes and saw eternity. Suddenly, I knew who walked with me all my life, who whispers my name in the night, who spoke to me and who put forgiveness in my heart. It was my gracious Lord.

Before John died, I told him about dying and coming back. John knew I was telling the truth because I knew things that I never knew before. John told his friends that I died and came back. I think he believed what had happened to me. I forgave John for everything he did to me. Also, before my mother died, she asked me to forgive her for what she did to me, and I forgave her. The Lord said, "But if ye forgive not men their trespasses, neither will your Father forgive your trespasses" (Matt. 6:15 KJV).

I loved my mother and John; I miss them very much. When I went to sit with my mother before she died, I knew from the way she looked at me that she was sorry for what she did to me. It's really too bad that people wait until they are dying to make it right with their loved ones.

I have tried to do what the Lord asked of me. I tell everyone about the love and the peace of the Lord Jesus, and about Him coming back soon. I tell everyone not to be discouraged, afraid, or hopeless about things that happen, but that we must learn, in all things, to turn to the Lord. He is our strength and salvation. He is always carrying us in unbearable times in our lives. He will carry our burden when we feel that we just can't carry on. His strength begins when ours ends. He hears our cries and our prayers, and reaches down from heaven to lift us up into His arms. We must learn to trust, obey, and accept His will in all things.

I will praise His name forever, until the day I can go home again to my Lord in heaven. It is sometimes hard for me to be here, but I feel His love and peace all around me every day. I don't know when He is coming back. He didn't tell me the exact time or the place. He just said, *"Tell the people—soon! I will return soon!"* I know all the signs are in place. He could return anytime, so everyone should get ready and prepare a place for Him in their lives. The Lord said, "But of that day and hour knoweth no man, no, not the angels of heaven, but my Father only" (Matt. 24:36 KJV).

As a lasting sign of His words to me, that wonderful Christmas and every Christmas since, my flowers and pussy willow bush bloom. In the heart of winter, with freezing snow and ice, my yard is in bloom with life—as a living symbol that the Lord will return soon to claim His people. Every year I call the television stations about my miracle of blooming flowers. WKJG Channel 33 and WANE Channel 21 have been out several times to film this miracle in the snow. No footprints have appeared since that first Christmas, but there are beautiful flowers blooming in my yard. I feel I am fulfilling the Lord's mission for me by letting everyone know of the yearly Christmas miracle in my yard. This last Christmas, the news reporters were so impressed that they actually took some of my bloomed lilacs and pussy willow branches back to the station and showed them live on the air, Christmas Day, 1997. One of them said it was indeed a miracle.

I now try and do good works for the Lord, and I suggest other people do this also. If everyone would do just one good deed a day, just think what the world would be like.

One day, I went to the laundry because my water softener was not working. I was sitting in my car when a van drove up beside my car. A man and a woman were in the van, and it was full of dirty clothes. The woman said to her husband, "I won't have enough soap for all these clothes! We will just have to make do and use just a little bit of soap for each load."

It looked like they had approximately twenty loads of laundry to do. The woman told me her washer was broken, and, with a large family, she had waited to do her laundry all at once.

As I sat in my car the Lord told me, *"Give this woman a box of soap and thirty dollars."* I really did not have thirty dollars to spare, but the Lord always provides for me. So I took the soap and the thirty dollars into the laundry, and I told the woman that the Lord wanted her to have some help.

I gave it to her, and as I left, she said, "Thank you! At least, tell me your name."

I said, "I'm Helen," and I left. Sears came and fixed my water softener, so I did not go to the laundry again. I know the Lord sent me there that particular day to help those people.

One day I went to a garage sale and bought a handbag. When I got home, I was looking in the handbag and I found three twenty-dollar bills. I knew I had to take the money back to the woman. So I did, and she thanked me so much. The next day she put an ad in the paper. She wanted to find me for a reward, but I never answered the ad. The "thank you" was enough for me.

I know the Lord is always with me, guiding me and helping me when I need it. I see the North Star blinking at me as a reminder that He will always be with me. I can see His face in the clouds. I hope you find this story of the Lord's miracle to be as amazing as I do. I know that at this time in history people are searching for answers and need miracles to reaffirm their faith and confidence in our Lord and Savior. I think time is running out—the Lord is about to return for His people. The Lord is the one who wanted this book published, so all people can see His footprints and blooming flowers and believe.

I hope the Lord comes back by the year 2000—this world is getting worse and worse. With all the floods, fires, droughts, and other natural disasters, not to mention all the crimes and other terrible things happening to people, God is saying to us all, *"Get ready for My return."* The Lord loves all people and wants them on His side. The devil is working overtime right now because he knows his time is running out soon. I want everyone to see heaven.

I know this story will be hard for some people to believe. Sometimes I can't believe what has happened to me. But you can believe the Lord can do miracles. The Lord at this time needs His people to help Him here on earth, to do His will. It won't be long until all of us will see more miracles and we will be with the Lord Jesus forever in heaven. Won't that be wonderful? No more bills to pay, no more illness, no more death—just heaven. Prepare a place for Him in your heart and in your soul, for He said to me, *"I will return soon!"*

People need the Lord—at the end of broken dreams, during times of illness and sorrow, when feeling sad or alone or frightened. You can turn to the Lord, and He will carry you though all the trials and tribulations in your life. The Lord also needs you to share with Him when your heart is filled with the wonderful things that happen in your life, the times when your soul is filled with joy, peace, and happiness. Always keep the Lord in front of you, keep your eyes on His footprints, and follow Him.

My sister Judy took this picture Christmas Day, 1986, to document the miracle.

Christmas Day, 1997: The pussywillow bloomed again.
What a miracle in the snow!

This picture of the Lord's footprints was taken on Christmas Day, 1983.

Footprints in the Sand

One night a man had a dream that he was
walking along the beach with the Lord.
Across the sky flashed scenes from his life.
For each scene, he noticed two sets of footprints in the sand;
one belonging to him, the other belonging to the Lord.

When the last scene of his life flashed before him,
he looked back at the footprints in the sand.
He noticed that many times along the path of his life
there was only one set of footprints,
and that it happened at the very lowest
and saddest times in his life.

This really bothered him,
and he questioned the Lord about it.
"Lord, You said that once I decided to follow You,
You'd walk with me all the way.
But during the most troublesome times in my life,
there is only one set of footprints.
I don't understand why when I needed You most
You would leave me."

The Lord replied, "My precious, precious child.
I love you, and I would never leave you.
During your times of trial and suffering,
when you see only one set of footprints,
it was then that I carried you."
—Anonymous

February 26, 1984: This was taken during the
time I was in heaven.

Christmas Day, 1997: The pussywillow was in full bloom, and look at all the snow! I'm holding the actual photograph taken in 1983 of the Lord's footprint.

To order additional copies of

My Walk with Jesus

Send $11.99* plus $3.95 shipping and handling to

Helen Bechtel
P.O. Box 8556
Fort Wayne, IN 46898-8556

e-mail: Hbec313486@aol.com

Indiana residents add 5% sales tax